CASE UNSOLVED FILES

CASE No. 003 THE GARDNER

This book is dedicated to
the men & women who
have worked this case.

Photograph credits pages 94–95: Getty Images.

Balzer + Bray is an imprint of HarperCollins Publishers.
HarperAlley is an imprint of HarperCollins Publishers.

Unsolved Case Files: The 500 Million Dollar Heist: Isabella Stewart
Gardner and Thirteen Missing Masterpieces

Library of Congress Control Number: 2022933119
ISBN 978-0-06-299158-4 — ISBN 978-0-06-299157-7 (pbk.)

The artist used pens, pencils, and Adobe Photoshop to create the
illustrations for this book.
Typography by Tom Sullivan and Dana Fritts
24 25 26   GPS   10 9 8 7 6 5 4 3 2

First Edition

UNSOLVED CASE FILES

THE 500 MILLION DOLLAR HEIST

Isabella Stewart Gardner
and Thirteen Missing Masterpieces

by TOM SULLIVAN

BALZER + BRAY
Imprints of HarperCollins Publishers

THIS IS A TRUE STORY.

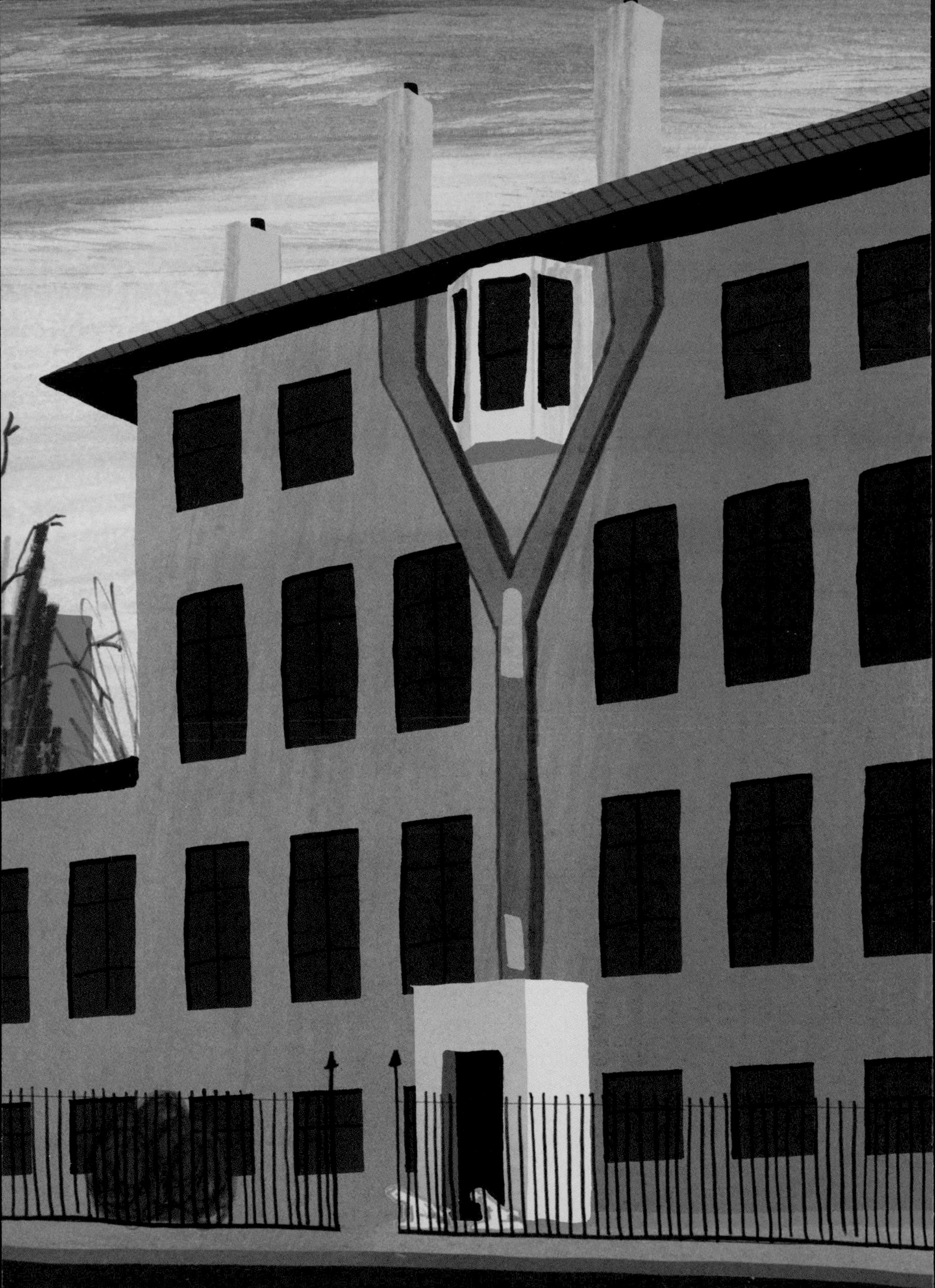

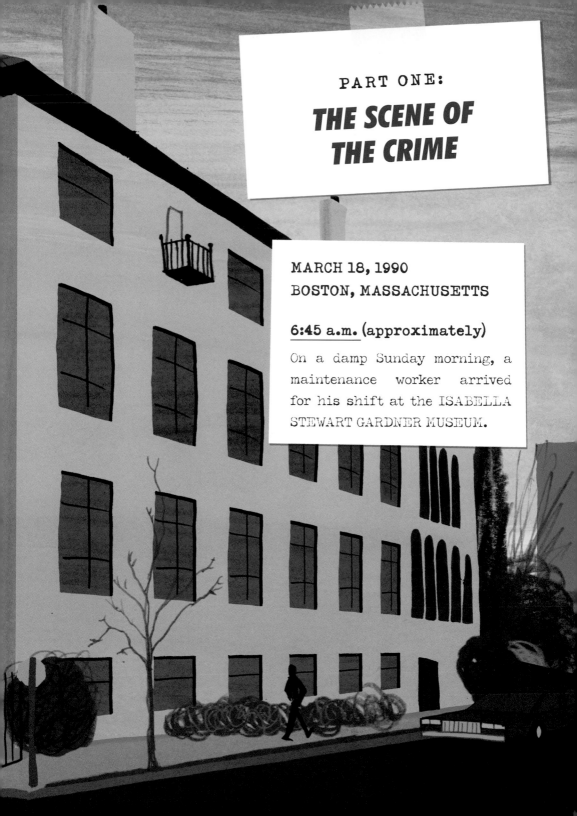

PART ONE:
THE SCENE OF THE CRIME

MARCH 18, 1990
BOSTON, MASSACHUSETTS

6:45 a.m. (approximately)

On a damp Sunday morning, a maintenance worker arrived for his shift at the ISABELLA STEWART GARDNER MUSEUM.

As usual, the worker approached the side entrance to the museum off PALACE ROAD and rang the bell to be buzzed in.

But there was no response.

A museum guard named KAREN SANGREGORY arrived at the Palace Road entrance for her shift, only to find the maintenance worker still locked out. The overnight guards were supposed to let them into the building. But after they'd repeatedly rung the bell and knocked on the windows, it became apparent that something was wrong.

SANGREGORY hurried across the street to a nearby college dormitory, where she found a pay phone and called her supervisor.

In the early 1990s, most people did not carry cell phones. If someone needed to make a call while away from home, they used a pay phone, which could be found all over most cities and towns, on the street or inside buildings. Local calls cost a nickel up until the 1950s, a dime into the 1970s, and by the 1990s, a phone call typically cost a quarter.

After around ten minutes, security supervisor LARRY O'BRIEN arrived with a passkey, and the trio entered the building through the garden. The museum was dark, and there was no one seated at the security desk, as there should have been at all times.

The group headed for security director LYLE GRINDLE'S office, where they found the door kicked in and the room in complete disarray. Papers were scattered, videotapes were missing, and on the desk chair was an empty picture frame.

In a panic, O'BRIEN picked up the phone and dialed 911. He then phoned GRINDLE and informed him that there had been a robbery. GRINDLE instructed O'BRIEN not to let anyone else into the museum except for the police.

The museum's director, ANNE HAWLEY, who at the time had been on the job for only a few months, was eating breakfast when she received a frantic call from GRINDLE.

Boston Police detective sergeant PAUL CROSSEN was driving on the Southeast Expressway when the call came in over the radio.

And acting curator KAREN HAAS was walking toward the museum for what she thought would be a quiet Sunday morning at work. But when she turned the corner, she was shocked to find half a dozen squad cars with flashing lights in front of the building.

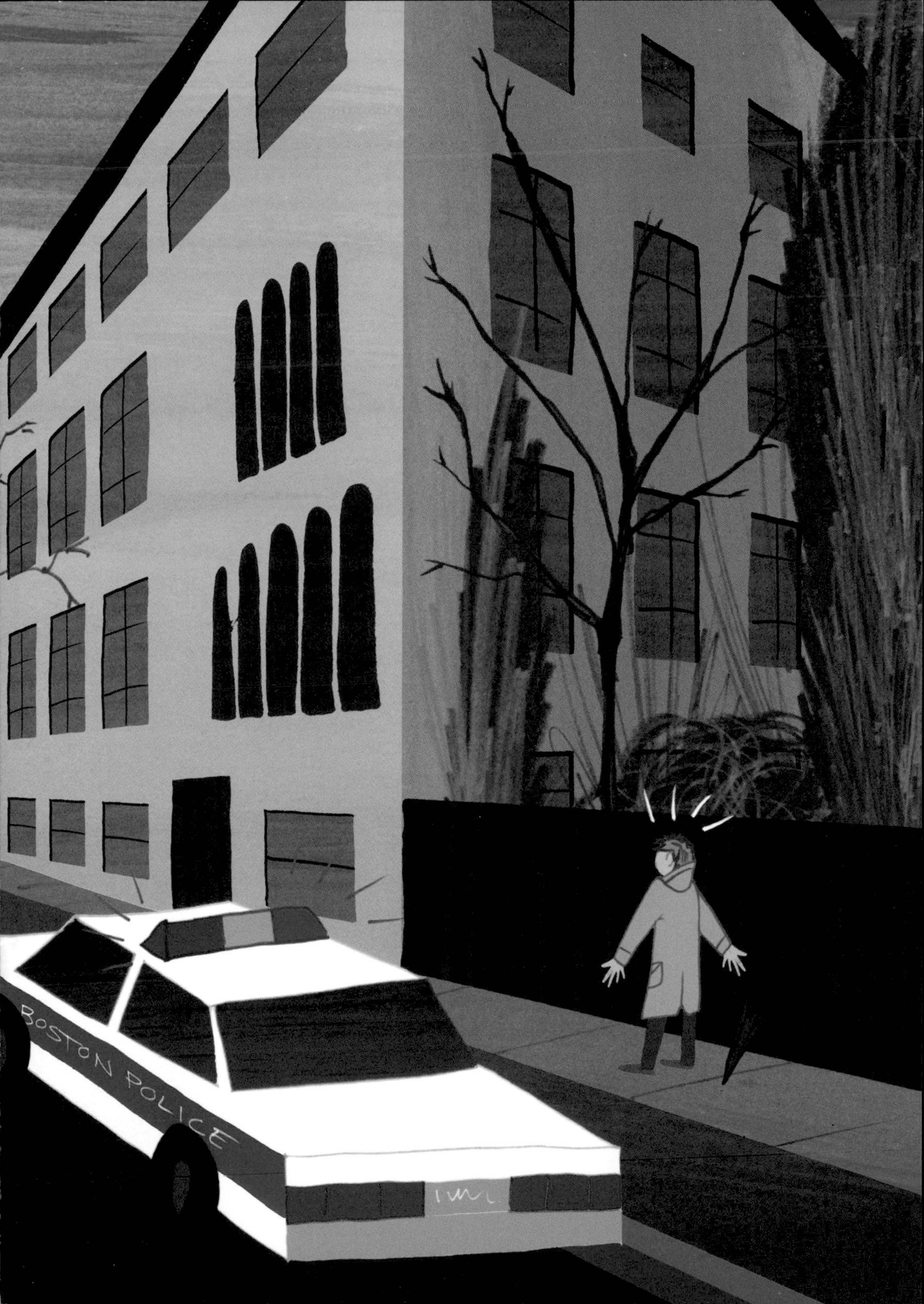
BOSTON POLICE

Detective CROSSEN led a team of Boston Police officers up to the fifth-floor attic. They didn't know if the intruders were still inside the building, or where the night guards were—if they were even still alive. So with guns drawn, the police officers searched every gallery, closet, and hidden nook as they worked their way down through the building floor by floor. Room by room, they hurried past broken glass and discarded picture frames in search of the missing men.

After more than twenty minutes, the police officers finally made their way into the basement.

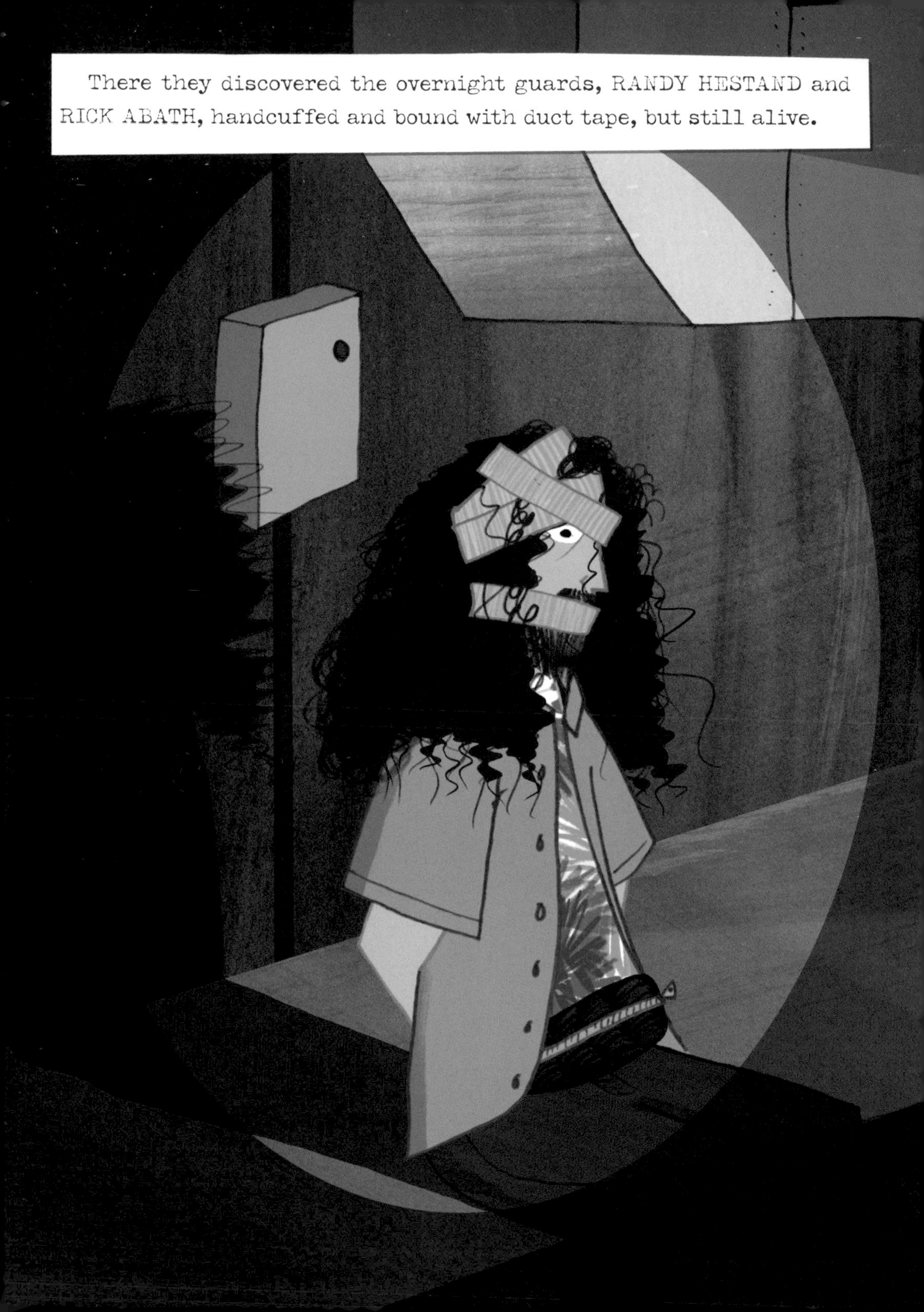
There they discovered the overnight guards, RANDY HESTAND and RICK ABATH, handcuffed and bound with duct tape, but still alive.

Soon the normally quiet streets outside the museum were bustling with FBI agents, city and state police, paramedics, and members of the bomb squad.

And the Dutch Room, which housed some of the museum's most prized possessions, was roped off with barricade tape as the central scene of the crime.

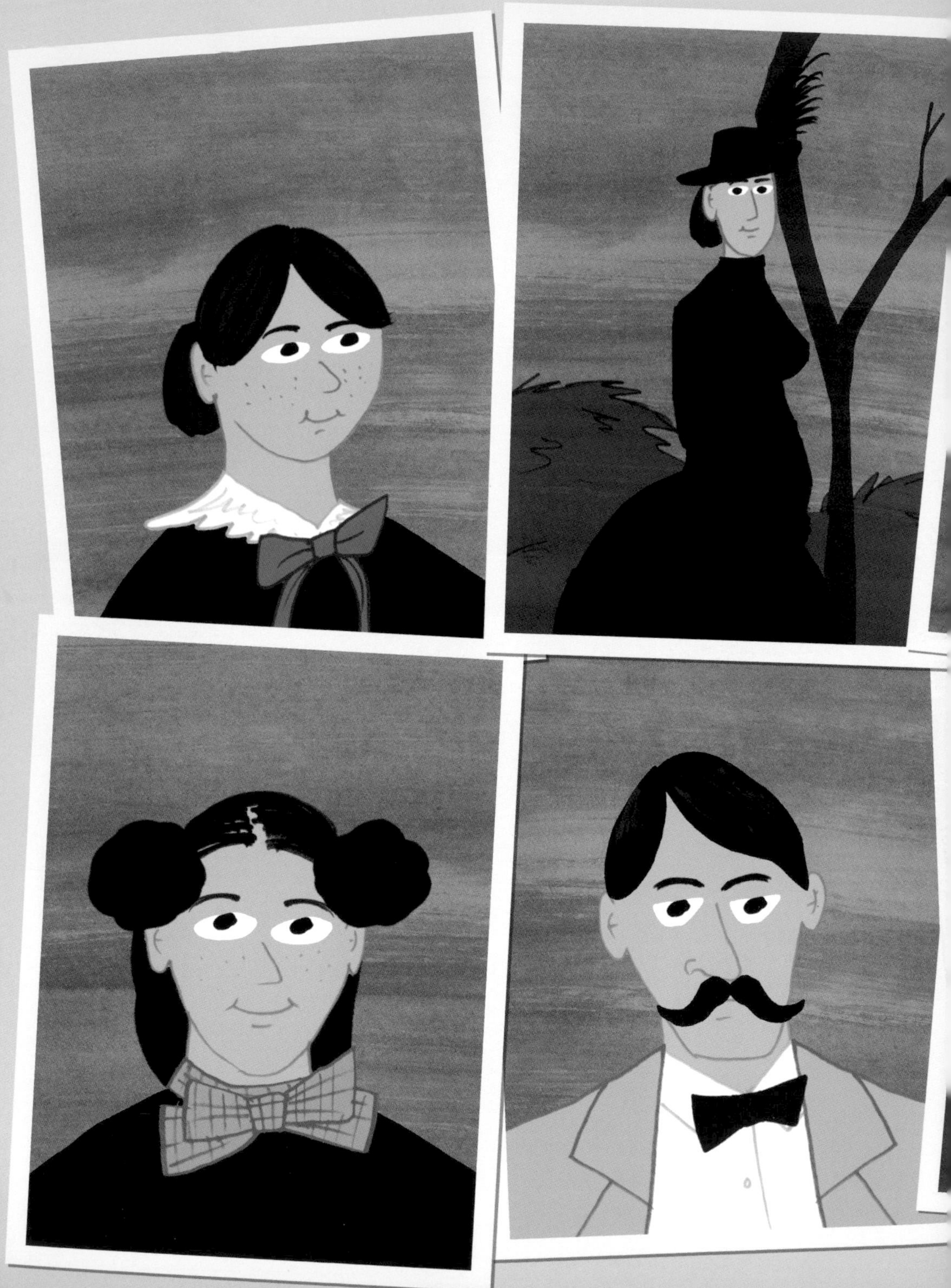

PART TWO

FENWAY COURT

ISABELLA STEWART was born in NEW YORK CITY in 1840, and as a teenager she visited MILAN, ITALY, which is where she first dreamed of one day founding her very own museum. At the age of nineteen she married the wealthy businessman JOHN LOWELL GARDNER JR. in Boston. The couple had a son, who sadly died of pneumonia before the age of two. Afterward ISABELLA descended into a deep depression, and upon the advice of a doctor, she and her husband traveled to EUROPE, where her love of art rekindled her spirit.

Upon her return to Boston, ISABELLA became a fixture of the local newspaper gossip columns. She was often spotted wearing slim Parisian dresses rather than the prim and proper gowns that were customary among New England socialites at the time.

15

ISABELLA traveled the globe, riding elephants and racing cars.

She gambled with the men at the local racetrack, and once caused quite a stir when she attended the symphony sporting a headband celebrating the BOSTON RED SOX'S 1912 World Series victory.

On trips to EUROPE, the MIDDLE EAST, and ASIA, she amassed a large collection of paintings and sculptures. At one auction she famously outbid the LOUVRE MUSEUM in PARIS and the NATIONAL GALLERY in LONDON to become the proud owner of JOHANNES VERMEER'S *The Concert*. ISABELLA sometimes smuggled her paintings back to America to avoid paying export taxes she could easily afford.

In 1891, her father, the wealthy linen merchant DAVID STEWART, died, and she inherited $2.1 million, which would be well over $50 million in today's money. She vowed to spend it all on art. In 1898, her husband passed away, and within weeks she had purchased the land for her museum.

ISABELLA based the design of the building on the PALAZZO BARBARO in VENICE, ITALY, but she flipped the design scheme inside out, so that the elaborate architectural features faced in toward a garden courtyard rather than decorating the exterior of the building.

She named her museum FENWAY COURT, and spent a year arranging her collection of over 300 paintings, nearly 400 sculptures, and thousands of antiquities. Every object in the museum was carefully placed so as to evoke emotion and invite conversation.

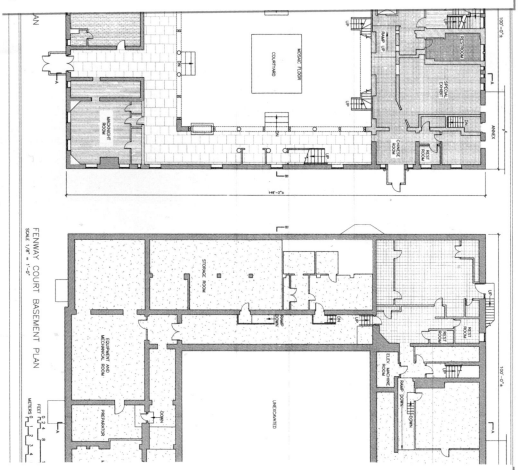

The museum opened its doors on New Year's Day 1903 and was met with rave reviews. ISABELLA lived on the fourth floor of the museum until her death on July 17, 1924, after which the building was renamed for its founder.

NATIONAL PARK SERVICE
U.S. DEPARTMENT OF THE INTERIOR

FENWAY COURT (ISABELLA STEWART GARDNER MUSEUM)
280 THE FENWAY   BOSTON   SUFFOLK COUNTY   MASSACHUSETTS

MA-1334

HISTORIC AMERICAN
BUILDINGS SURVEY
SHEET 3 OF 15 SHEETS

In her strict will, GARDNER stipulated that the collection was never to be rearranged, and that nothing was ever to be added to or removed from the museum. If anything was, the entire collection was to be auctioned off and the proceeds donated to HARVARD UNIVERSITY.

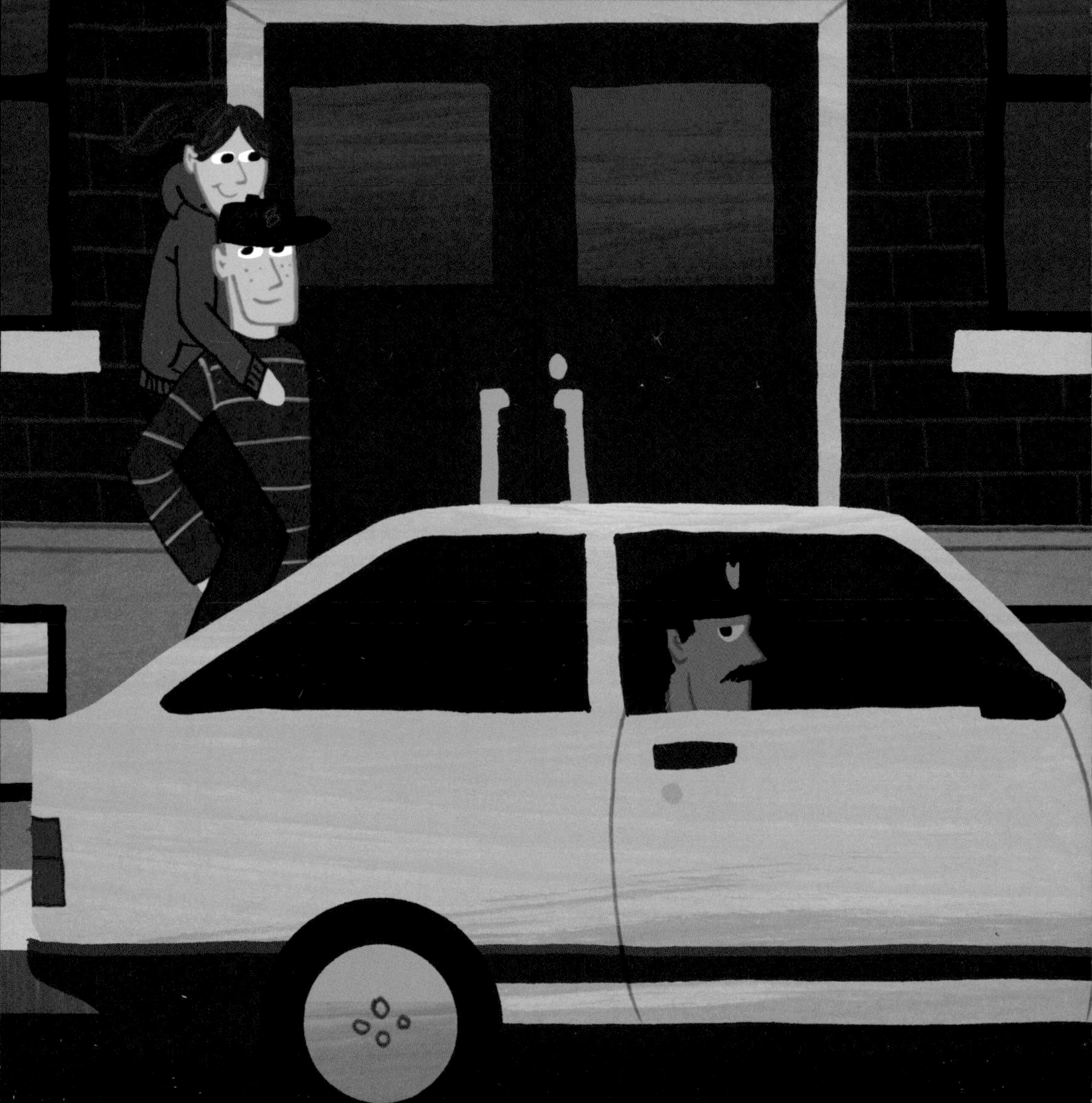

PART THREE:
COPS & ROBBERS

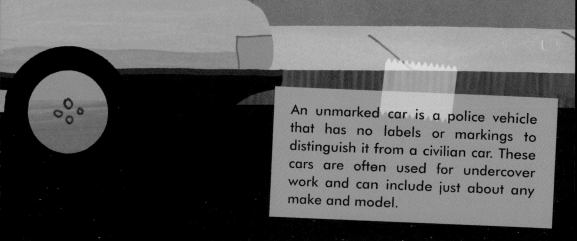

MARCH 18, 1990
<u>**12:45 a.m.**</u>

A couple of high school students left a Saint Patrick's Day party and meandered down Palace Road. As they made their way toward the Isabella Stewart Gardner Museum, they noticed what appeared to be two police officers sitting in an unmarked car.

An unmarked car is a police vehicle that has no labels or markings to distinguish it from a civilian car. These cars are often used for undercover work and can include just about any make and model.

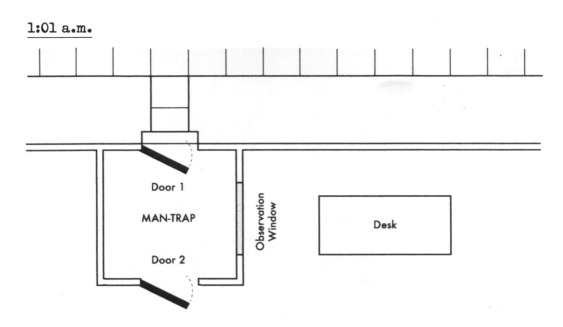

Inside the museum, night watchman RICK ABATH—dressed in a tie-dyed shirt and a Stetson cowboy hat—was finishing his rounds. But before he relieved RANDY HESTAND from his post at the security desk, ABATH opened the security door, went through the man-trap, and opened and closed the exterior door—allegedly to ensure that the door was locked securely.

A man-trap is the space between two separate locking doors, like an ATM lobby at a bank. Usually each door will have its own unique lock, with the space in between acting as an added security measure.

Security protocol dictated that one guard would be seated at the security desk at all times while the other patrolled the museum. The guard on patrol would walk through all the rooms and galleries in the museum, turning security keys in the alarm locks around the building. This activity was recorded on a security printout.

ABATH then took his seat at the security desk, and HESTAND, armed with a flashlight and a radio, began his rounds. A few moments later, ABATH watched on the video monitor as the security camera outside the building recorded a hatchback pulling up and parking near the entrance.

1:24 a.m.

Two mustachioed Boston Police officers approached the entrance and rang the buzzer. One of them looked directly into the camera above the door and said, "Police. We're here about the disturbance."

03/18/1990
01:24:13

ABATH wasn't aware of any disturbance on the grounds, but against protocol, he buzzed them in through the man-trap. Normally the guard on duty would record the names and badge numbers of any police officers attempting to gain entry to the museum, then call Boston Police headquarters to verify the officers' identities.

The shorter of the two cops asked the guard if he was alone. ABATH told them that RANDY HESTAND was out on his rounds, and the police officers asked him to summon his partner. But just as ABATH called HESTAND on his walkie-talkie, he noticed that the mustache on the taller officer appeared to be fake.

Then the shorter police officer told ABATH that he looked familiar, and that they might have a warrant out for his arrest, so they instructed the guard to step out from behind the desk—away from the panic button.

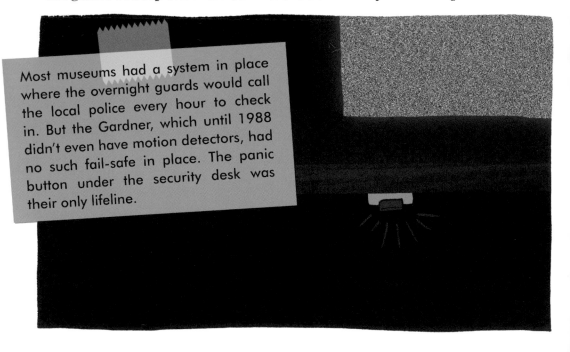

Most museums had a system in place where the overnight guards would call the local police every hour to check in. But the Gardner, which until 1988 didn't even have motion detectors, had no such fail-safe in place. The panic button under the security desk was their only lifeline.

The shorter police officer shoved RICK ABATH up against the wall and slapped a pair of handcuffs on him. As ABATH was asking why they were arresting him, RANDY HESTAND walked into the room. The larger of the two police officers grabbed and handcuffed him before saying, "This is a robbery. Don't give us any problems and you won't get hurt."

The thieves wrapped the men's heads haphazardly in duct tape, covering their eyes and mouths, then wordlessly brought the guards into the basement. They handcuffed HESTAND to a sink and led ABATH down a dark hallway, where they handcuffed him to a workbench.

The thieves rifled through the guards' pockets and removed their wallets. After examining their driver's licenses, the men told the guards, "We know where you live. Do as we say and no harm will come to you. Don't tell them anything, and in about a year you'll get a reward."

The thieves ascended the main staircase to the second floor and walked past the majestic Venetian courtyard on their way to the Dutch Room and REMBRANDT VAN RIJN'S *Christ in the Storm on the Sea of Galilee.*

At just over five feet long and four feet wide, the painting is a shining example of the Dutch master's range as an artist.

But as the robbers reached for it, a high-pitched alarm broke the silence. Startled, one of the thieves ran over and smashed the motion detector. As the room fell quiet once again, they carefully removed the large painting from its hangers.

The thieves then hurled the heavy frame onto the hard tiled floor, shattering the protective glass.

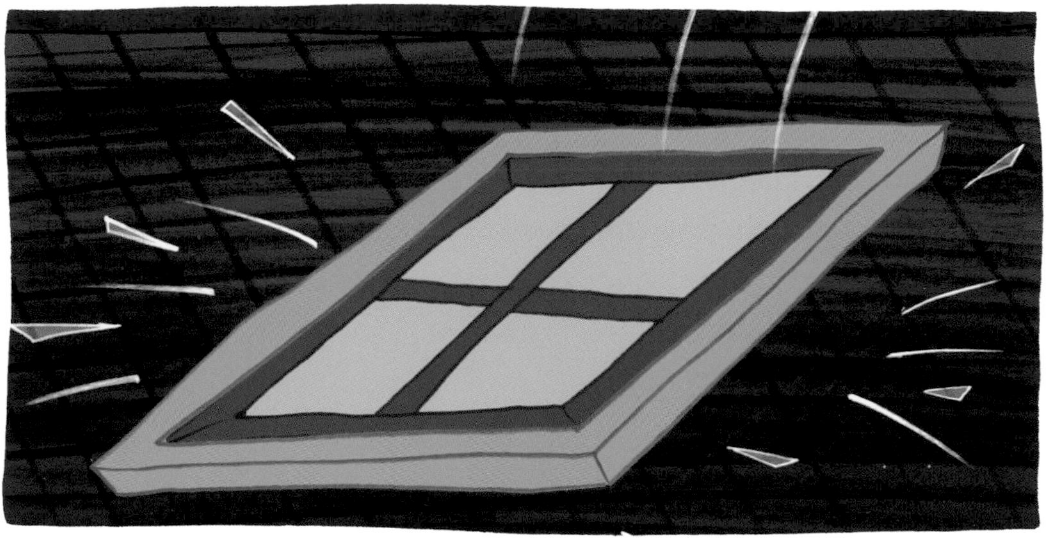

One of the men, brandishing a blade, slashed the priceless 357-year-old painting, ripping the heavily varnished canvas from its wooden backing.

They then did the same to REMBRANDT'S *A Lady and Gentleman in Black.*

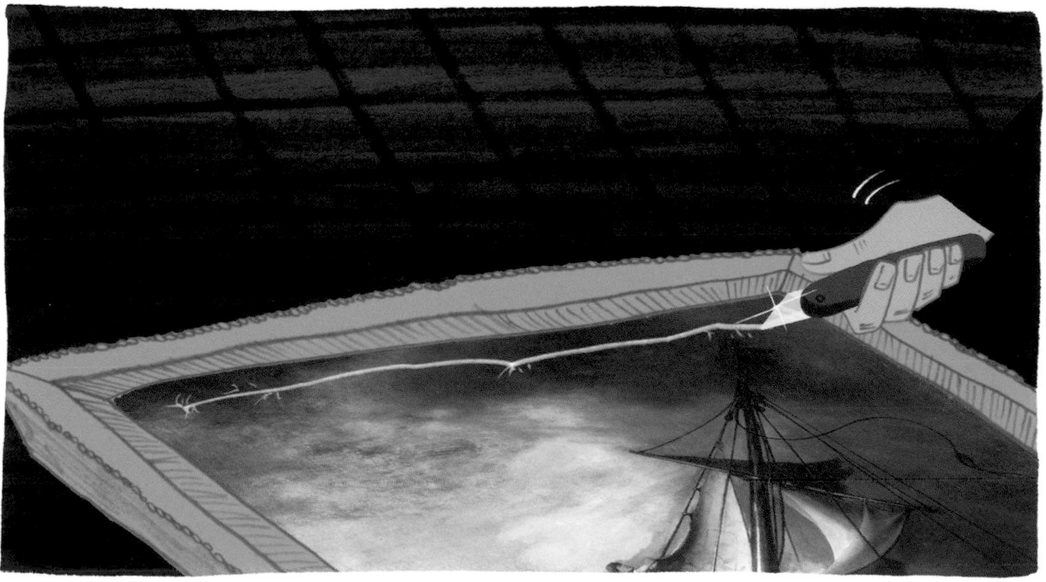

One of the thieves went back down the hallway, through the Early Italian Room and the Raphael Room, into the Short Gallery, where the thief smashed the frames holding five sketches by the French Impressionist EDGAR DEGAS.

Back in the Dutch Room, the other thief removed a large self-portrait of REMBRANDT that was completed when the great painter was only twenty-three. Perhaps it was simply too big, or maybe the thief just had second thoughts about taking it—either way, the painting was left unscathed, leaning up against the wall.

Instead, the crook took a small, etched self-portrait of REMBRANDT that was barely larger than a postage stamp.

The thief then removed GOVAERT FLINCK'S *Landscape with an Obelisk* from its position on an observation desk by the window.

Meanwhile, the robber in the Short Gallery had turned his attention toward a framed flag once carried by NAPOLEON BONAPARTE'S French Imperial Army. Curiously, rather than smashing the frame to pieces as they had with the others, the thief removed six of the screws holding it together before abandoning it and instead making off with a 10-inch gilded bronze eagle finial that had once stood atop the flag as it was waved in battle.

The burglar in the Dutch Room snatched JOHANNES VERMEER'S *The Concert*, which experts believe is the most valuable item taken that evening, and perhaps the most expensive item ever stolen in the world.

The Concert had its protective glass shattered and was removed from its frame, but the painting was spared the slashing that the two Rembrandts endured.

The last item that the thieves pilfered from the Dutch Room was a bronze gu from the Shang Dynasty. The twelfth-century-BC Chinese beaker was the oldest of all the items stolen that night.

While one of the thieves went back down to the basement to check on the guards, the other entered the Blue Room, located on the museum's ground floor.

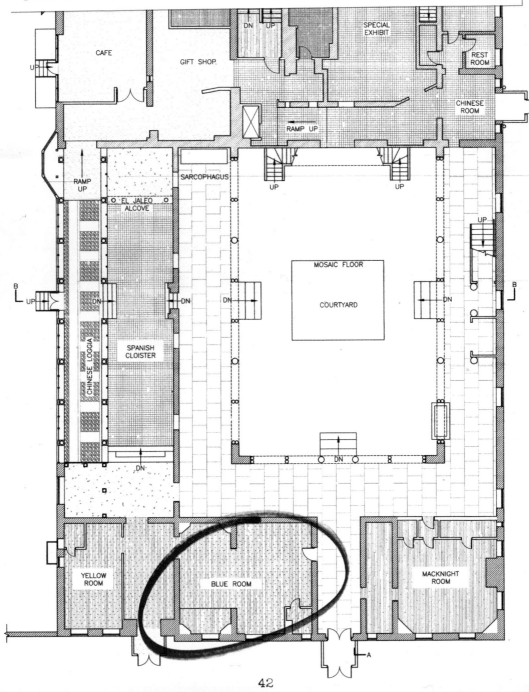

There he took a small oil portrait, *Chez Tortoni* by ÉDOUARD MANET.

Strangely, this was the only object taken from the first floor.

The thieves then made their way to the security director's office, where they brutally kicked in the door. The men took the VHS tapes out of the security video recorder, removing the only visual evidence of their identities.

They then took the security printouts, which had been logging
distress calls from the sixty-plus motion detectors scattered around
the museum. The thieves were apparently unaware that the data was
also recorded on a hard drive that they left behind.

```
Date: 03/18  Time: 01:54  Panel: 02 P2
Alarm Point:  09  DUTCH ROOM              Status:  ALARM
!SOMEONE IS IN THE DUTCHROOM. INVESTIGATE IMMEDIATELY!!!


Date: 03/18  Time: 01:54  Panel: 02 P2
Alarm Point:  09  DUTCH ROOM              Status:  NORMAL
!SOMEONE IS IN THE DUTCHROOM. INVESTIGATE IMMEDIATELY!!!



Date: 03/18  Time: 01:55  Panel: 02 P2
Alarm Point:  09  DUTCH ROOM              Status:  ALARM
!SOMEONE IS IN THE DUTCHROOM. INVESTIGATE IMMEDIATELY!!!



Date: 03/18  Time: 01:55  Panel: 02 P2
Alarm Point:  09  DUTCH ROOM              Status:  NORMAL
!SOMEONE IS IN THE DUTCHROOM. INVESTIGATE IMMEDIATELY!!!



Date: 03/18  Time: 01:55  Panel: 02 P2
Alarm Point:  09  DUTCH ROOM              Status:  ALARM
!SOMEONE IS IN THE DUTCHROOM. INVESTIGATE IMMEDIATELY!!!



Date: 03/18  Time: 01:55  Panel: 02 P2
Alarm Point:  09  DUTCH ROOM              Status:  NORMAL
!SOMEONE IS IN THE DUTCHROOM. INVESTIGATE IMMEDIATELY!!!



Date: 03/18  Time: 01:55  Panel: 02 P2
Alarm Point:  09  DUTCH ROOM              Status:  ALARM
```

And as if to thumb their noses at the museum's security director,
the culprits left the empty frame that had once housed *Chez Tortoni*
sitting on his chair.

The security system recorded the outside doors opening and closing, indicating that one of the thieves had left the building.

2:45 a.m.

After being inside the museum for a total of eighty-one minutes, the second thief left the building. With his arms full of stolen artifacts, he climbed into the hatchback, and the two drove off into the night with their haul.

Once the men were gone, all that remained were scattered paint chips, threads of canvas, shards of glass, and denuded picture frames—reminders of the great masterpieces that once lived inside them.

PART FOUR:
THE LOOT

The Concert
Johannes Vermeer
1663–66
Oil on canvas
28 9/16 x 25 1/2 in.

At the time of the theft, the thirteen stolen pieces were valued at roughly $200 million. They're now believed to be in the $500 million range, although the exact worth is impossible to estimate since they were purchased so long ago, and there are no recent comparable sales to help determine their value. But it's said that *The Concert* could be worth upward of $250 million on its own.

By the time of his death at forty-three in 1675, JOHANNES VERMEER had only completed thirty-four or so paintings—an exact number is unknown, and often disputed. In the world of museum-quality fine art, there is probably nothing rarer to a collector than a VERMEER.

REMBRANDT VAN RIJN'S works are no stranger to theft, with one of his paintings, *Jacob de Gheyn III*, having been stolen on four separate occasions since 1966, earning it the nickname "takeaway Rembrandt."

Christ in the Storm on the Sea of Galilee
Rembrandt van Rijn
1633
Oil on canvas
63 x 50 3/8 in.

Scholars believe REMBRANDT completed close to 300 paintings, but only one seascape: *Christ in the Storm on the Sea of Galilee*.

A Lady and Gentleman in Black was a portrait commissioned by an unknown wealthy couple. Art historians found out that at one point there had been a small child standing next to the woman, but after the boy's presumed death, his image was painted over.

A Lady and Gentleman
in Black
Rembrandt van Rijn
1633
Oil on canvas
51 13/16 x 42 15/16 in.

Portrait of the Artist as a Young Man was acquired alongside *Self-Portrait, Age 23*, in 1896, and were the first two REMBRANDTS that ISABELLA STEWART GARDNER ever purchased.

Portrait of the Artist as
a Young Man
Rembrandt van Rijn
Circa 1633
Etching
1 3/4 x 1 15/16 in.

GARDNER didn't collect many landscapes, but she made an exception for REMBRANDT, even though it was later determined that *Landscape with an Obelisk* was actually created by one of REMBRANDT'S followers, GOVAERT FLINCK.

Landscape with an Obelisk
Govaert Flinck
1638
Oil on panel
21 7/16 x 27 15/16 in.

Chez Tortoni
Édouard Manet
Circa 1875
Oil on Canvas
10 1/4 x 13 3/8 in.

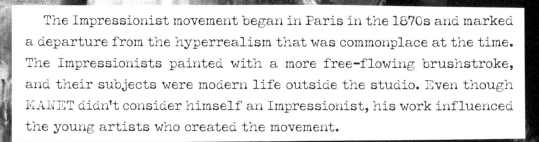

The Impressionist movement began in Paris in the 1870s and marked a departure from the hyperrealism that was commonplace at the time. The Impressionists painted with a more free-flowing brushstroke, and their subjects were modern life outside the studio. Even though MANET didn't consider himself an Impressionist, his work influenced the young artists who created the movement.

EDGAR DEGAS was not a fan of the term Impressionist, yet he is considered to be one of the founders of the movement. DEGAS'S muse was motion, and he regularly painted dancers, performers, and racehorses.

Leaving the Paddock
(La sortie du pesage)
Edgar Degas
19th century
Watercolor and pencil
on paper
4 1/8 x 6 5/16 in.

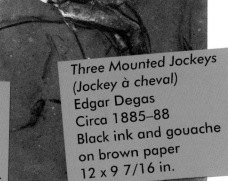

Three Mounted Jockeys
(Jockey à cheval)
Edgar Degas
Circa 1885–88
Black ink and gouache
on brown paper
12 x 9 7/16 in.

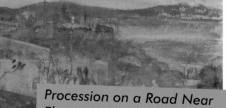

Procession on a Road Near
Florence (Cortège sur une route
aux environs de Florence)
Edgar Degas
1857–1860
Pencil and sepia wash on paper
6 1/8 x 8 1/8 in.

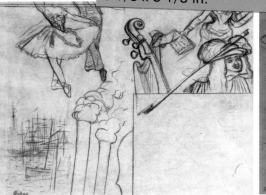

Study for the programme de la
soirée artistique du 15 Juin 1884 (2)
Edgar Degas
1884
Black chalk on paper
9 11/16 x 12 3/8 in. & 10 1/2 x 14
13/16 in.

Modeled after the work of sculptor ANTOINE-DENIS CHAUDET, the Napoleonic finial that once stood atop the imperial battle flag has its own separate reward of $100,000 for information leading to its recovery. With more historical than artistic importance, some believe the bronze eagle was swiped by one of the thieves as a keepsake.

Eagle Finial: Insignia of the First Regiment of Grenadiers of Foot of Napoleon's Imperial Guard
After Antoine-Denis Chaudet
1813–1814
Gilded bronze
10 in.

The twelfth-century-BC Chinese ritual vessel called a gu was traditionally used for wine. While it was one of the oldest works in the collection, it is not as valuable as some of the pieces that the thieves might have stolen, leading some to think that this was also pilfered as a keepsake.

Beaker (Gu)
Chinese, Shang Dynasty
12th century BC
Bronze
10 7/16 x 6 1/8 in.

News of the theft rocked the art world, and to this day it remains the single largest private property theft in the United States. Shortly after, at the urging of the FBI, a reward of $1 million was offered for information leading to the safe return of the stolen objects.

After interviewing RICK ABATH and RANDY HESTAND, a police sketch artist created drawings of the suspects—with and without mustaches.

DESCRIPTION:
WHITE MALE
LATE 20'S TO EARLY 30'S
DARK EYES DARK HAIR
HEIGHT: 5'-7" to 5'-10"
MEDIUM BUILD
GOLD WIRE RIM GLASSES

The sketches were released to media outlets, but ABATH declared that the drawings were "awful" and looked nothing like the men in question.

Authorities believe that the suspects had inside information, or an accomplice with intricate knowledge of the museum. They cite the fact that once the men entered the museum, they led the guards into the basement without asking where the staircase was.

DESCRIPTION:
WHITE MALE
EARLY TO MID 30'S
DARK EYES DARK HAIR
HEIGHT: 6' to 6'-1"
WEIGHT: 180 - 200

Some people have even placed that blame on ABATH. He did break protocol by allowing the men to gain entry into the building. He also opened the outside door prior to their arrival—a possible signal to the men that the coast was clear—but this evidence is circumstantial.

There are, however, the bizarre details surrounding *Chez Tortoni*.
Displayed on the first floor of the museum in the Blue Room, the portrait by ÉDOUARD MANET was the only object stolen from that location. Although the museum's motion detectors were able to timestamp the whereabouts of the thieves during their raid, there is no indication that they went near, let alone inside, the Blue Room.

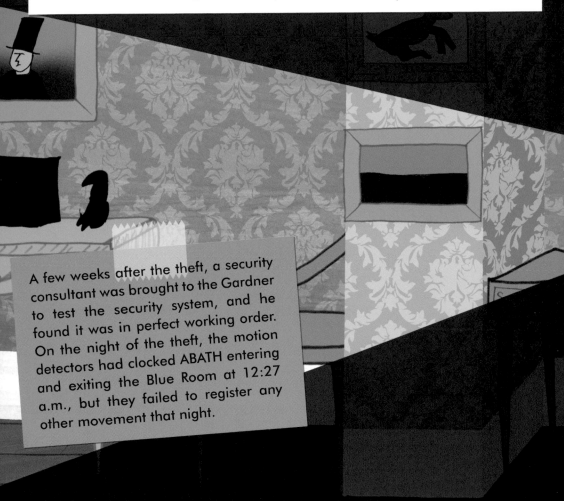

A few weeks after the theft, a security consultant was brought to the Gardner to test the security system, and he found it was in perfect working order. On the night of the theft, the motion detectors had clocked ABATH entering and exiting the Blue Room at 12:27 a.m., but they failed to register any other movement that night.

And it was *Chez Tortoni*'s frame that was left behind on LYLE GRINDLE'S office chair. The security director was ABATH'S boss, and coincidentally, ABATH had handed in his two weeks' notice shortly before the robbery.

According to his coworkers, however, the idea that the twenty-three-year-old music school dropout would help orchestrate a massive art heist—and in the process swipe a masterpiece for himself—was a little farfetched. As incriminating as the circumstances surrounding the theft of the MANET are, the fact remains that ABATH was not some criminal mastermind; he was simply the best that the museum could afford.

Unlike the nearby MUSEUM OF FINE ARTS, which employed ex-police officers as guards and had a top-of-the-line security system, the Gardner paid college students minimum wage, didn't have insurance, and hadn't even installed the motion detectors until two years before the theft. It wasn't so much a matter of *if* the museum would get robbed, but *when*.

While the FBI chased leads, and days turned into weeks and then months, all the museum could do was sit back and hope that the reward money would be enough to make someone talk.

But it wasn't.

The museum board of trustees has also stepped up its efforts to recover the art treasures, upping the reward it's offering for the safe return of all items in good condition from $1 million to $5 million.

After seven fruitless years, the museum upped the reward from one million to five, and within a few months they had their first big break in the case.

AUGUST 13, 1997
DEDHAM, MASSACHUSETTS

A small-time crook named WILLIAM P. YOUNGWORTH III caused quite a stir when he declared to the press, from the steps of the courthouse, that he could broker the return of eleven of the thirteen missing pieces of art.

All that he wanted in return was to have the current charges against him dropped, immunity from any charges stemming from the Gardner heist, the $5 million reward, and for his friend MYLES J. CONNOR JR. to be released from federal prison.

The son of a police officer, MYLES CONNOR was a former rock musician who had played with the Beach Boys. He robbed his first museum at age twenty, and after robbing a woman's home in 1965, he famously broke out of the HANCOCK COUNTY JAIL in MAINE by carving a gun from a bar of soap and painting it with shoe polish.

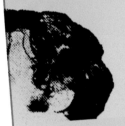

JIM McGETTRICK'S
BEACHCOMBER
PHONE: 479-8989
Wollaston Beach Blvd., Quincy

AY AFTERNOON
N-ROLL AGAIN with
ES CONNOR
esident of Rock-n-Roll

Connor

show u

for a c

Jury acquits Myles Connor

If had he not been in prison on March 18, 1990, he would have been
the prime suspect in the Gardner case. After all, he had gotten out of
jail once before by brokering the return of a stolen REMBRANDT.

At around noon on April 14, 1975, MYLES CONNOR, disguising his red hair under a brown wig and leather chauffeur's cap, purchased tickets to Boston's Museum of Fine Arts (MFA) along with an associate. The two men walked right up to REMBRANDT'S *Portrait of a Girl Wearing a Gold-Trimmed Cloak* and brazenly removed the 17 x 23-inch oval painting from the wall.

A guard tried to stop the men, but they brandished a firearm, and the guard relented. Another guard was pistol-whipped when he attempted to stop them. More guards came running, but CONNOR and his associate fired bullets at their feet before taking off in a waiting car.

There's almost no market for a stolen REMBRANDT, or any masterpiece, since the item is simply too well-known. However, CONNOR found that a high-profile stolen painting can make for an effective bargaining chip.

While facing a fifteen-year sentence for trying to fence N. C. WYETH paintings, CONNOR brokered the return of the MFA's missing REMBRANDT (that he himself had stolen) and was able to cut his sentence down to four years. All of a sudden the rumor was born that if you could return a stolen masterpiece, you were essentially handed a get-out-of-jail-free card.

To "fence" is to knowingly purchase stolen goods at below market value and then resell them for a profit.

The authorities brushed off YOUNGWORTH'S claims as a likely hoax, since he was a known con man. But the bold declarations intrigued TOM MASHBERG, a reporter for the *Boston Herald*, so he reached out to YOUNGWORTH.

After some back and forth, YOUNGWORTH called MASHBERG late one evening and agreed to show him proof that he did indeed have control of the items. Just before midnight on August 17, 1997, YOUNGWORTH picked up MASHBERG from the *Boston Herald* offices. The deal was simple: YOUNGWORTH would show MASHBERG proof, then the reporter would have to wait a week before he could write the story for the paper. That way YOUNGWORTH would have the chance to move the paintings to another secure location.

After a few hours, the pair arrived at a storage facility in an industrial area of RED HOOK, BROOKLYN.

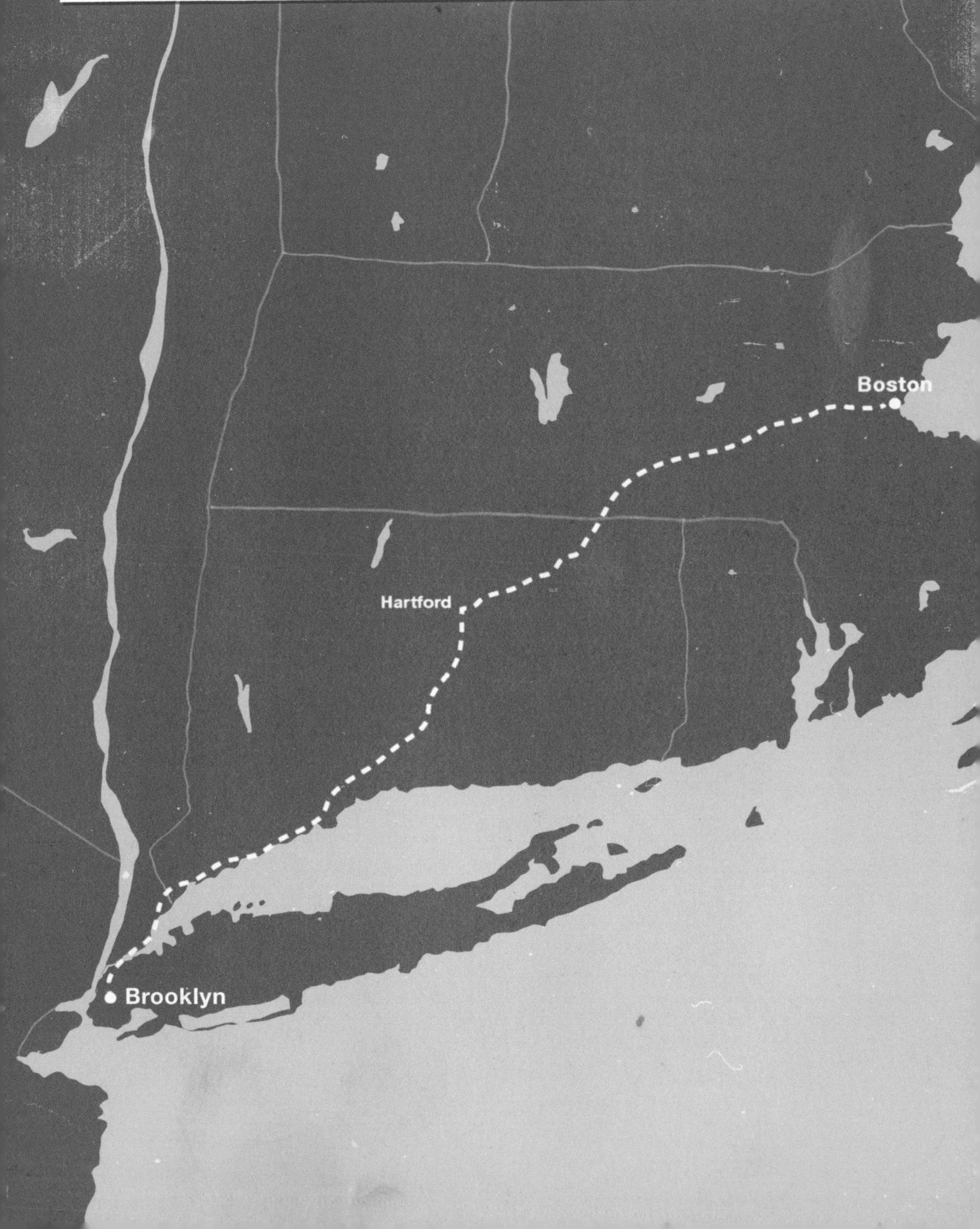
Boston
Hartford
Brooklyn

YOUNGWORTH led MASHBERG up four flights of stairs and down a dark hallway. Once there, he opened a padlocked door and entered the room.

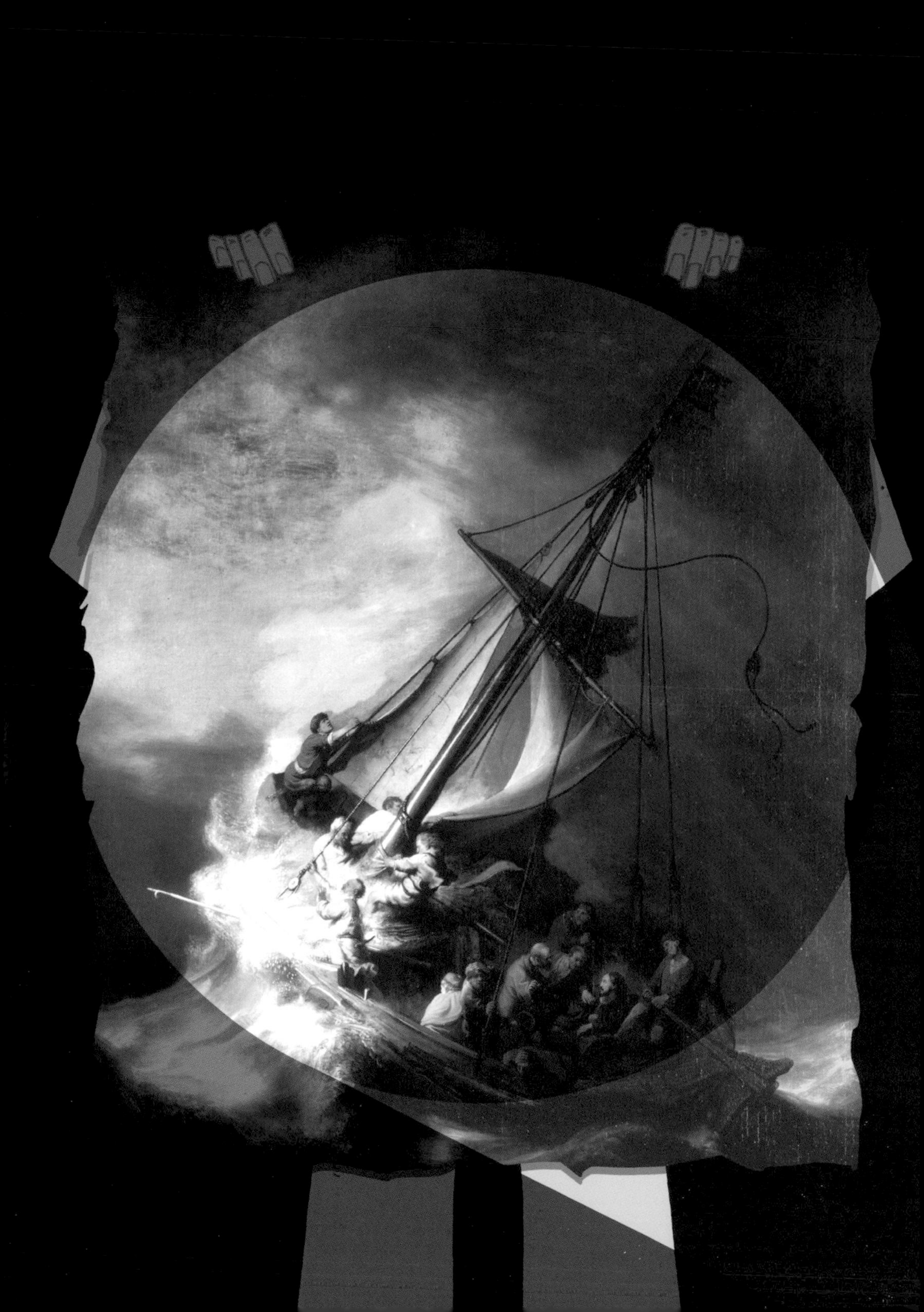

We've seen it!

In the dim light, YOUNGWORTH put on gloves and removed a large black cardboard mailing tube from one of many plastic bins. He then carefully unrolled *Christ in the Storm on the Sea of Galilee*. MASHBERG could see the frayed edges from where it had been sliced out of its frame, he could make out the cracks in the canvas, and he could see REMBRANDT'S signature on the rudder of the ship. But then he was quickly whisked away from the storage locker and placed in a cab.

A week later, the *Herald* ran the story on the front page, with a headline exclaiming, "We've seen it!"

MASHBERG was then contacted by the Gardner's chief conservator, BARBARA MANGUM, and was asked to describe what he had witnessed that night in the storage locker. The frayed edges, cracks, and signature all lined up, but some questioned whether the painting would even physically be able to be rolled up since it was so heavily coated in protective varnish.

If the authorities were going to cut a deal with YOUNGWORTH, they'd need "proof of life."

After a couple of months, a plain manila envelope arrived at the *Boston Herald*'s offices. Inside were low-quality (and ultimately inconclusive) photographs of the paintings, but there was also a small vial containing paint chips. The paint chips were examined by WALTER C. MCCRONE, a CHICAGO-based scientist who specialized in examining evidence under electron microscopes. MCCRONE was able to determine that the paint chips were roughly 350 years old, and that they originated in HOLLAND.

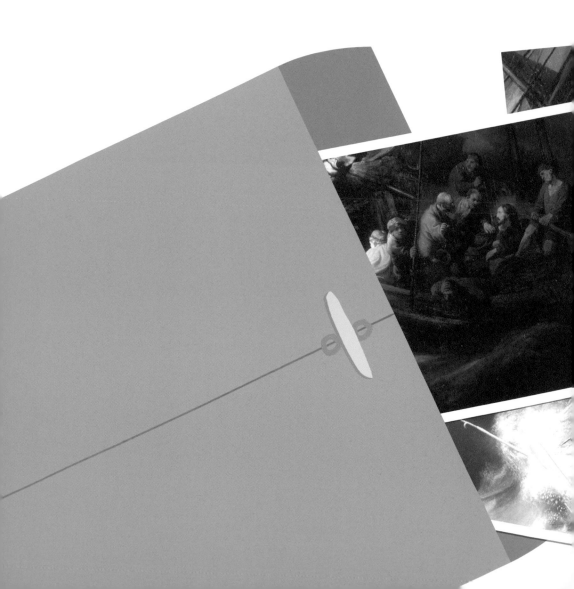

However, museum officials decided to conduct their own examination of the paint chips and determined that they were not from either of the REMBRANDTS. At the urging of TOM MASHBERG, the chips were tested against the VERMEER, and while they were determined to be potentially consistent with *The Concert*, it was already too little, too late. YOUNGWORTH was labeled a fraud in the press and sent to jail, and the FBI lost interest in cutting a deal.

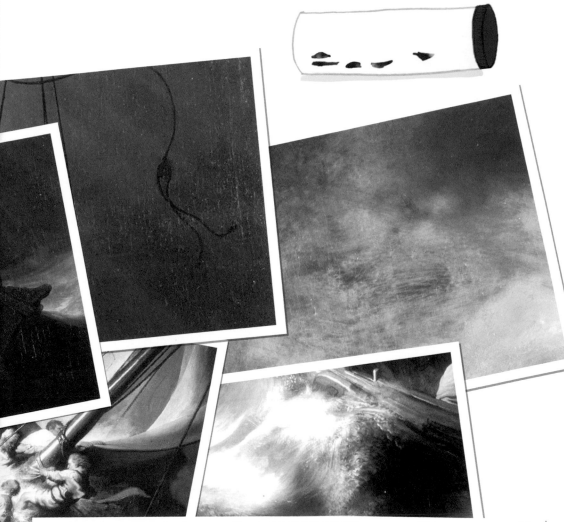

There's a good chance that YOUNGWORTH was pulling a con all along, but if not, how did he come to be in possession of the artwork to begin with?

According to MYLES CONNOR, he and his friend ROBERT "BOBBY" DONATI had cased the Gardner Museum as far back as the early 1970s. And CONNOR even claims that during one of their trips to the museum, DONATI had taken a liking to the Napoleonic eagle finial, while CONNOR himself favored the Shang Dynasty gu—the two items supposed to have been keepsakes for the thieves.

During his lifetime of crime, MYLES CONNOR had amassed an impressive collection of ancient samurai swords and artwork large enough to fill a 40-foot trailer. When he was jailed in 1989, he trusted an old friend and fellow criminal to look after his belongings. But when that man decided to leave his life of crime behind, he passed CONNOR'S collection to YOUNGWORTH for safekeeping.

YOUNGWORTH gradually sold off MYLES CONNOR'S collection. Perhaps attempting to facilitate CONNOR'S release from prison was his way of making amends. But in any case, no one can say for certain how, or *if*, YOUNGWORTH was ever actually in possession of the stolen artwork.

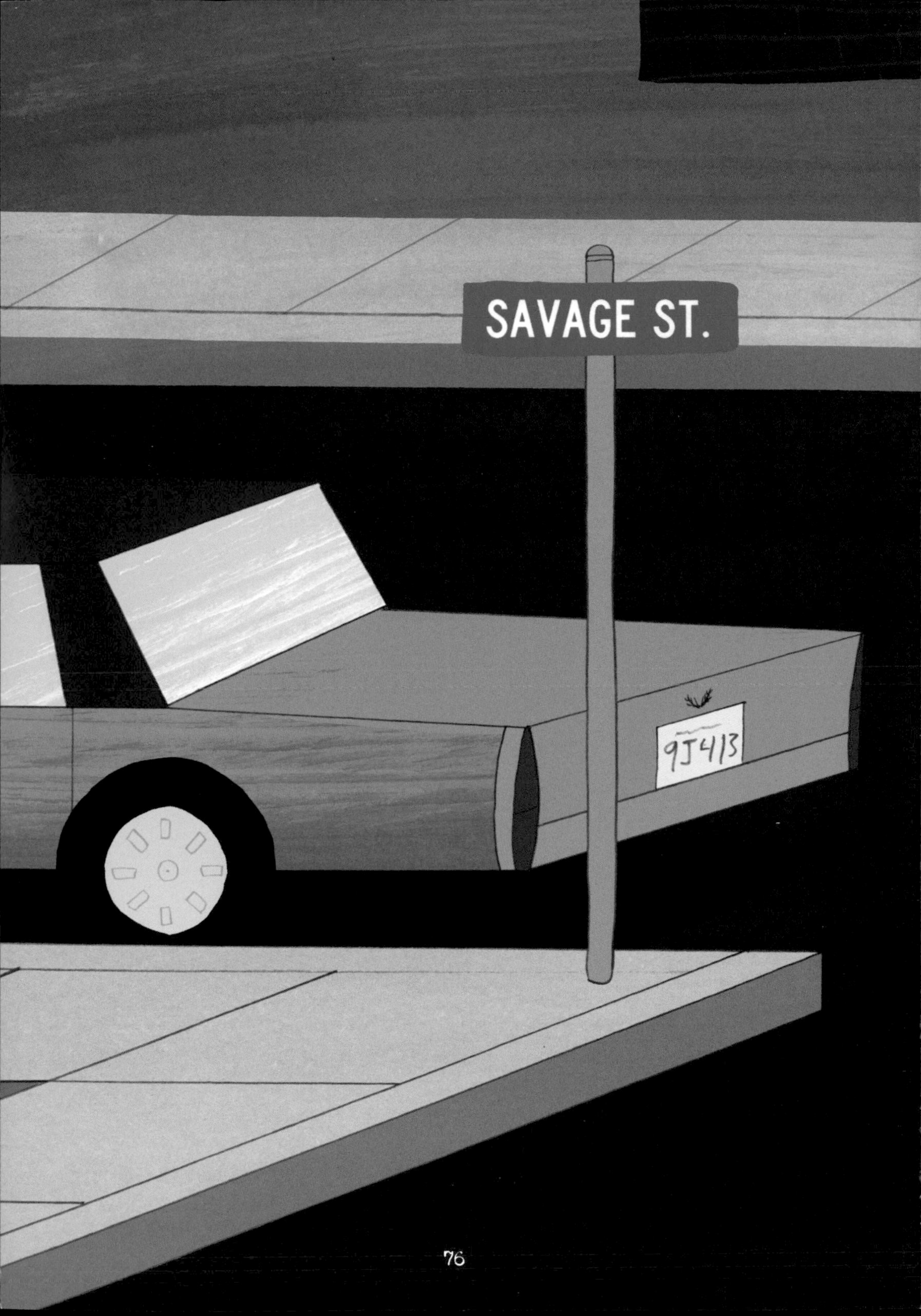
SAVAGE ST.
9J413

PART SEVEN

A TANGLED WEB

Revere man found slain in trunk of his car

In September of 1991, BOBBY DONATI was found dead in the trunk of his car. If he had in fact been involved with the theft, any hope investigators had of obtaining a confession died with DONATI. But as investigators looked deeper into his mob ties, a theory emerged.

Some believe that since DONATI didn't match any descriptions of the thieves, he must have hired the job out, possibly to a trusted colleague, fellow mobster ROBERT GUARENTE. In fact, DONATI had been seen a few days before the robbery with GUARENTE at a bar in REVERE, MASSACHUSETTS, allegedly carrying a bag that contained police uniforms.

M. CONNOR

R. DONATI

W. YOUNGWORTH

les Connor held

hout bail

GUARENTE'S associate CARMELLO MERLINO ran an auto-body repair shop in the DORCHESTER neighborhood of Boston as a front. Every crook in Boston knew that if you were looking for anything from an unmarked gun to a 350-year-old Dutch masterpiece, the guys at TRC AUTO ELECTRIC had a way of obtaining it.

A "front" is a legitimate business, such as a garage, a bar, or a construction company, that is run by criminals. They use the legitimate business as a way to hide—or "launder"—the money that they earn through their criminal enterprises.

R. GUARENTE

C. MERLINO

TRC AUTO

According to police reports, a lot of people came and went from TRC AUTO ELECTRIC, but "no one was getting their car fixed." And two of the regulars, DAVID TURNER and GEORGE REISSFELDER, just happened to match the physical descriptions of the Gardner suspects.

A year after the heist, in March of 1991, REISSFELDER was discovered in his home, dead from an apparent drug overdose. He largely remains a person of interest in the robbery due to the fact that two of his relatives claim that they saw MANET'S *Chez Tortoni* hanging above his bed. But when the authorities searched his apartment, there was no sign of the painting.

G. REISSFELDER

CHEZ TORTONI

Four are
with coca

Witness kille

According to the FBI, only about 5 percent of stolen artwork is ever recovered. But even after all this time, the museum has still not given up hope.

If you or your family have any knowledge of the whereabouts of these thirteen missing pieces of art, please contact your local FBI office.

Federal agents search for the missing art at the Manchester, Connecticut home of ROBERT GENTILE.

The empty frames that once housed VERMEER'S *The Concert* and REMBRANDT'S *Christ in the Storm on the Sea of Galilee*.

PHOTOS FROM THE FILES

ANNE HAWLEY, the museum's director, answers questions from the press on March 19, 1990.

Museum conservationists collect scattered paint chips from REMBRANDT'S *A Lady and Gentleman in Black*.

As a reminder of the theft, and because GARDNER'S will forbade the acquisition of any new paintings, the empty frames still hang on the gallery walls, serving as hopeful beacons that the paintings will one day be returned.

In 2017, the Isabella Stewart Gardner Museum raised the reward for information leading to the recovery of the missing artwork to $10 million.

But the thirteen priceless pieces of art have never been recovered.

Investigators have followed up leads all over the world, with reported sightings in SAUDI ARABIA, CANADA, IRELAND, FRANCE, COLOMBIA, JAMAICA, and JAPAN.

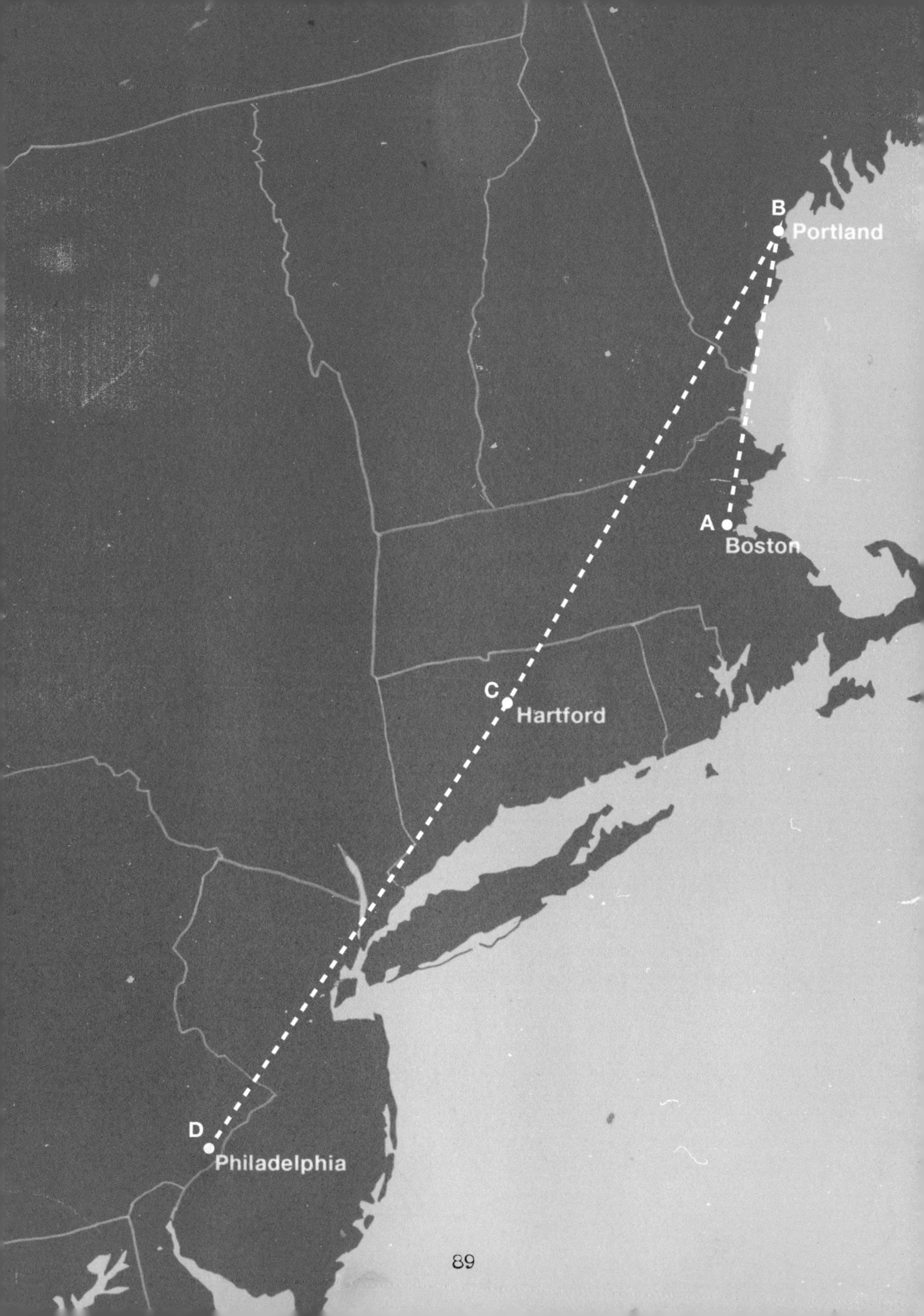
B
Portland
A
Boston
C
Hartford
D
Philadelphia

On March 18, 2013, the twenty-third anniversary of the heist, the FBI announced that they believed the paintings had been moved from Boston to Maine, and then down to Philadelphia via Connecticut. They then claimed to know who had committed the robbery, and that the men were now dead, but they didn't want to share the suspects' names because until the paintings were recovered, it was still an active investigation.

Inside the house, however, federal officials did find an old copy of the *Boston Herald* with a front-page story about the theft, and a handwritten list of all the stolen artwork with estimated "street values" for the paintings. While that is an incredibly incriminating coincidence, it's also circumstantial.

THE CONCERT	$ 10 MILLION
STORM ON THE SEA	$ 8 MILLION
LADY + GENTLEMAN	$ 2 MILLION
CHEZ TORTONI	$ 500 THOUSAND
LANDSCAPE w/ OBELISK	$ 500 THOUSAND
SELF-PORTRAIT	$ 200 THOUSAND
DEGAS SKETCHES	$ 50 THOUSAND

While facing jail time on the drug and weapons charges, GENTILE was offered immunity if he could produce the paintings—which he did not.

FEB 8, 1988: Burglars break through a skylight into the Colnaghi Art Gallery in New York City, and steal 27 Old Master paintings and drawings. The stolen artwork is valued at $6 million, including panels by 15th century Italian Renaissance master Fra Angelico.

In 2010, the FBI obtained a search warrant for GENTILE'S home in MANCHESTER, CONNECTICUT. During the search the feds found a secret compartment under his backyard shed, and inside was a large plastic bin. But it contained no art.

In 2002, ROBERT GUARENTE had lunch with his friend ROBERT GENTILE in PORTLAND, MAINE. According to GUARENTE'S wife, "one or more" of the paintings were given to GENTILE that day.

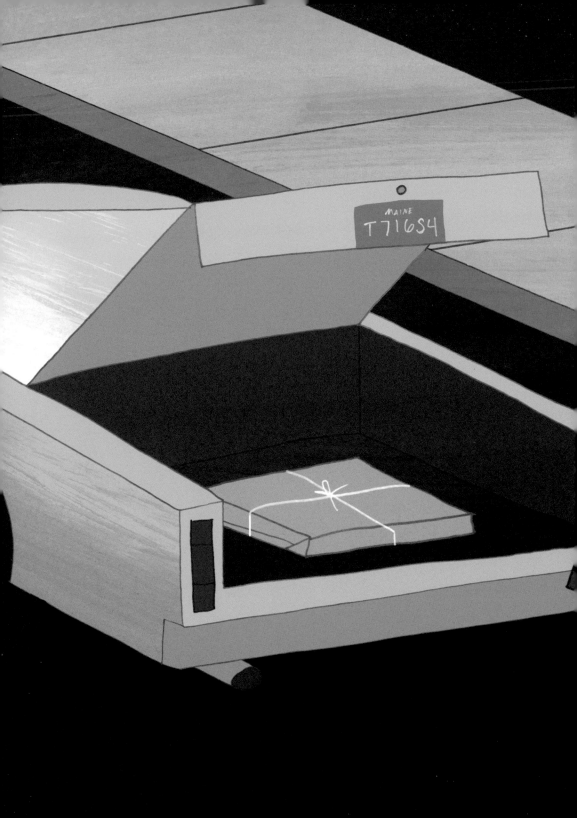

MAINE
T716S4

With the help of an informant, TURNER was finally apprehended in 1999, along with MERLINO and another associate, on their way to rob an armored-car facility. With TURNER facing upward of forty years in prison, it seemed that if he was ever going to exchange the paintings for his freedom, it would be now. But he maintained his innocence in the museum theft.

Even though he fit the physical description of one of the suspects, TURNER had an alibi for the night the Gardner was robbed. Credit card receipts placed him in MIAMI, FLORIDA—although a receipt produced for returning a rental car in FORT LAUDERDALE on March 20, 1990, had a different driver's license number, which suggests he may have manufactured his alibi.

```
MIAMI SPY
INTERNATIONAL

  255 E. FLAGER ST.
STE. 85 MIAMI, FL 33131
        377-2157

SUN 03/18/1990 11:43 AM

MERCHANT ID:      T071618
TERMINAL ID:      12

TRANSACTION ID:   #E9F47
TYPE:             CREDIT


      PURCHASE


NUMBER:    XXXXXXXXXXX8313
MODE:              SWIPE
CARD TYPE:         VISA


RESPONSE:      APPROVED
APPROVAL CODE: 5Q0PD457

SUB TOTAL:      $43.99
TAX:            $2.64
------------------------
                $46.63
TOTAL:


    THANK YOU
```

DAVID TURNER had been a standout high school athlete who gravitated toward a life of crime but somehow always managed to evade capture.

D. TURNER

harged

ne sales

C. PAPPAS

When CARMELLO MERLINO and an associate, CHARLIE PAPPAS, were indicted on cocaine charges in 1992, PAPPAS turned state's witness and began accusing his old friend and roommate DAVID TURNER of a number of crimes. But before charges could be brought up against TURNER, PAPPAS was gunned down at his fiancée's parents' house on the night before Thanksgiving.

SOURCES

All website URLs are accurate as of date of publication.

OVERVIEW OF THE CASE:

Barnicle, Colin, dir. *This Is a Robbery: The World's Biggest Art Heist.* New York: Tribeca Productions, 2021. Netflix.

Boser, Ulrich. *The Gardner Heist: The True Story of the World's Largest Unsolved Art Theft.* New York: Smithsonian Books, 2009.

"The Gardner Museum Theft." Federal Bureau of Investigation. March 18, 2013. www.fbi.gov/news/stories/5-million-reward-offered-for-return-of-stolen -gardner-museum-artwork.

Horan, Kelly, with reporting by Jack Rodolico. September–November, 2018, in *Last Seen*, produced by WBUR and the *Boston Globe*, podcast, MP3 audio, www .wbur.org/podcasts/lastseen/last-seen-season-one.

"Infographic: A Minute-by-Minute Look at the Gardner Museum Heist." *Boston*, March 2010. Updated March 18, 2013. www.bostonmagazine.com /arts-entertainment/2013/03/18/infographic-a-minute-by-minute-look-at-the -gardner-museum-heist/.

Isabella Stewart Gardner Museum. *Stolen.* Carlisle, MA: Benna Books, 2018.

Kurkjian, Stephen. *Master Thieves: The Boston Gangsters Who Pulled Off the World's Greatest Art Heist.* New York: PublicAffairs, 2015.

TOM MASHBERG'S EYEWITNESS ACCOUNT:

Mashberg, Tom. "Stealing Beauty." *Vanity Fair*, March 1998, https://archive .vanityfair.com/article/1998/3/stealing-beauty.

Mashberg, Tom. "We've Seen It! Informant Shows Reporter Apparent Stolen Masterpiece." *Boston Herald*, March 16, 2008. Updated November 17, 2018. www.bostonherald.com/2008/03/16/weve-seen-it-informant-shows-reporter -apparent-stolen-masterpiece/.